COMPLETE
MYST®
Hints and Solutions

by Paul Bodensiek

////IBradyGAMES

Legal Stuff

Complete Myst Hints and Solutions

Copyright ©1996

////IBradyGAMES

Brady Publishing
An Imprint of
Macmillan Computer Publishing
201 West 103rd Street
Indianapolis, Indiana 46290

ISBN: 1-56686-481-X
Library of Congress Catalog No: 95-080990

Printing Code: The rightmost double-digit number is the
year of the book's printing; the rightmost single-digit
number is the number of the book's printing. For example, 96-1 shows that the first printing of the book
occurred in 1996.

99 98 97 96   4 3 2 1

Manufactured in the United States of America.

////BradyGAMES *Staff*

Publisher
Rick Ranucci

Editor-In-Chief
H. Leigh Davis

Licensing Director
Maritza Gibbons

Development Team
Henly Wolin
Tim Cox

Project Editor
Tim Cox

Acquisitions Editor
Debra McBride

Screenshot Editor
Michael Owen

Technical Editor
Steve Zupan

Creative Director
Jean Bisesi

Book Designer
Kevin Spear

Production Team
Heather Butler
Dan Caparo
Dave Eason
Scott Tullis
Christine Tyner

About the Author

Paul Bodensiek has been a computer gamer since the days of the old TRS-80, not to mention the (quite possibly) millions of quarters he fed into Pong and Space Invaders machines. Now he plays just about any game he can find.

When not playing games, Paul runs ParaGrafix, a graphics design/writing/engineering firm he started because no one would pay him to do all the things he really likes. Interested in almost everything, he has also sailed as a crewmember aboard the *Mayflower* replica in Plymouth, Massachusetts, is working toward his pilot's license, and coauthored *Special Edition Using CorelDRAW! 5* for Que Corporation. Skydiving intrigues him, but the thought of jumping out of a perfectly good airplane just doesn't seem sane.

Paul is very lucky to share his life with his wife, Mary, and daughter, Melissa, who put up with his late nights working on this book.

You can reach Paul by email at **Paul@ParaGrafix.com**, or set your World Wide Web browser to **http://www.ParaGrafix.com**.

Complete Myst Hints and Solutions

Table of Contents

Chapter 1

Game Basics

The gameplay for Myst is rather simple. The common point-and-click technique lets you travel through the different Ages and interact with the items located throughout the eye-popping landscape of Myst Island. The basics of the game and setting up the game are described in the following sections.

The Controls

Basic Movement

Moving from location to location in Myst is very simple. If you need to walk forward, click straight ahead. If you need to walk left or right, click on the left or right side of the screen.

Details

You can even make 90 or 180 degree turns by moving the mouse to the left or right side of the screen. This occurs when the pointing hand (cursor) turns left or right, which indicates that clicking left or right will turn you in that direction.

Remember that some locations just are not accessible. If you click in a location and nothing happens, move on.

Interacting with Objects

To examine, use, or pick up an item, either click on it or click and drag the item. Clicking on an object either brings the object closer to you, or moves you closer to the object. If you click on a functional object, you may activate it or manipulate it.

You can also move levers and other objects by dragging them. You will know if you can drag an object because the pointing hand turns into a grabbing hand. This also occurs when you hold down the mouse button.

Shortcut Keys

There are several shortcut keys that you can use to quickly access different menu and file options.

ALT	Accesses the menu bar.
ALT-N (New Game)	Starts a new game. It's the same as if you double-clicked Myst for the first time.
ALT-R (Restore Game)	Allows you to access previously saved games.
ALT-S (Save Game)	Lets you save a game in progress.
ALT-F4 (Exit)	Exits your current game.
ALT-T (Transitions)	Toggles screen transitions on and off. You can navigate the game more quickly with the screen transitions off.
ALT-Z (Zip Mode)	Toggles Zip Mode on and off. When on, clicking an item when the cursor is a lightning bolt takes you directly to that area or object.
ALT-D (Drop Page)	Lets you drop a page you no longer need. When dropped, the page returns to the location from which it was originally picked up.

Installing the Game

To install Myst, do the following:

1. Start at the Windows Program Manager.

2. Insert the CD-ROM disc into your CD-ROM drive.

3. Choose **Run** under the **File** menu.

4. Type the following in the Command Line:

   d:\INSTALL.EXE (or the appropriate letter that designates your hard drive)

The install program then creates a default directory and copies the files from the CD into this directory. The program then creates a program item called "Myst" within a Windows group named "Broderbund Software." To run the game, double-click on the Myst icon.

Minimum System Requirements

Software	Windows 3.1; MS/PC-DOS 5.0 or higher
CPU	386DX, 33MHz (486 recommended)
RAM	4MB (8MB recommended)
Video	Super VGA graphics card (640×480×256)
CD-ROM	Required
Sound	Windows-compatible sound device

How to Use This Book

Myst is a complex and complicated game. Therefore, a hints book for this game should break down gameplay strategy into categories to make the information easier to use. That's just what this book does.

Complete Myst Hints and Solutions is divided into three user-friendly sections. Each Age has the following three sections: a Guided Tour, a Hints section, and a Solutions section. Each of these three sections are described below.

The Guided Tours

In contrast to the rest of the book, the Guided Tour is designed to give the gamer a quick journey of the entire game. The emphasis is on proceeding from Age to Age and ultimately to the end game.

In essence, the Guided Tours are divided into two sections. The first section describes a history or background of each Age. By contrast, the second section is a walkthrough that describes the layout of each Age and points out the significant areas in the Age that you'll encounter.

The Hints

If you're the type of player who wants to trudge through the whole game with only an occasional push to get you going in the right direction, this section is for you.

Each Age has its own Hints section. In each Age, some basic clues and hints are provided to lead you in the right direction, but don't necessarily tell you the solution to the puzzle. This section provides only the basics needed to steer you in the right direction enabling you to solve each puzzle on your own.

The Solutions

The Solutions section expands on the Hints by telling you exactly where you need to go, what items you may need to interact with, what path to take, and so on. You may not need this section for each puzzle, but it will come in handy when you find yourself at a loss for what to do next.

Chapter 2

Myst Island and the Library

"I realized the moment I fell into the fissure that the book would not be destroyed as I had planned... I have tried to speculate where it might have landed. I must admit, however, such conjecture is futile. Still, the question about whose hands may one day hold my Myst book is unsettling to me..."

The Myst Journal
Atrus

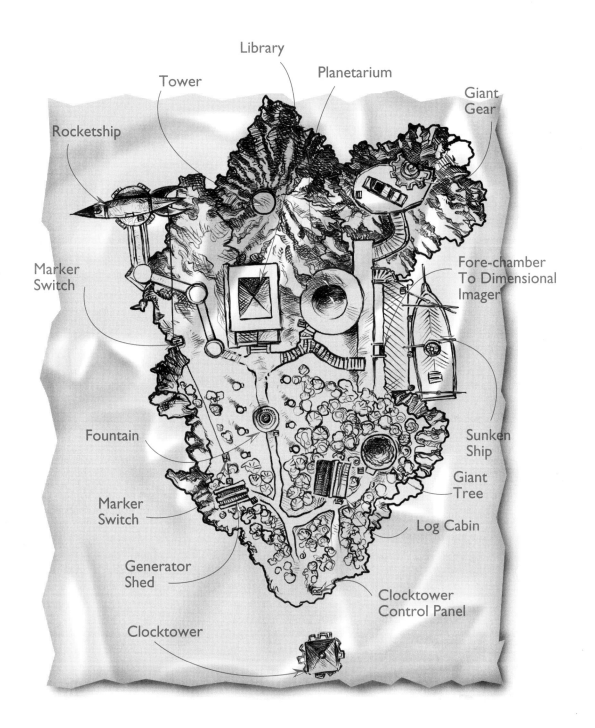

Rocketship

Tower

Library

Planetarium

Giant Gear

Marker Switch

Fore-chamber To Dimensional Imager

Fountain

Sunken Ship

Giant Tree

Marker Switch

Log Cabin

Generator Shed

Clocktower Control Panel

Clocktower

The History of Myst Island

Myst Island is a magical and mystical land full of beautiful landscapes and landmarks. But the intrigue…What about the different "Ages" that are supposed to be sealed within Myst Island? You can only wonder—or find out for yourself!

A Guided Tour

Myst Island is a serene, wondrous land filled with puzzling landmarks. To get your bearings straight, take a quick stroll along the pathway through the sites.

Your journey begins at the Dock. To your right, you'll see the remnants of a Sunken Ship, while to the left is a door that leads to an inner chamber of sorts.

Directly ahead of the Dock at the top of the hill are some Giant Gears. Just steps ahead, you'll notice a small domed building. Upon entering, you may think you've entered a futuristic dentist's office because you'll see a chair with a control panel in the center of the room.

The Library is probably the single most important landmark on the island. After you've gotten your bearings, head back here to begin your research.

In the distance, past the Library, the path leads to a launching pad with a Rocketship. A line of cables connects the Rocketship to an electrical tower.

Directly in front of the Library is the Pillar Walkway. It consists of a beautiful pool of water surrounded by a number of Pillars, each bearing a different symbol.

Continuing along the path, you'll notice a power station to the right that contains a Generator. Straight ahead, a great Clocktower rises high into the air.

Through the woods and to the left of the Clocktower is a Log Cabin. Inside you'll find a locked safe and a furnace. Finally, just behind the Log Cabin, stands a Giant Tree.

At this point, you may have some ideas about how these various pieces of the puzzle fit together or you may be totally baffled. Nevertheless, take heart and prepare to unravel the mystery of Myst. Your first stop: The Library.

The Hints

Alone, with only the sound of birds squawking and waves lapping, you find yourself confronted by a mysterious island. How will you find your way home? Where will you find the clues that unlock the secrets of Myst?

Myst Island requires a complete reconnaissance before proceeding. Explore, find what works, what doesn't, and what seems to work except for perhaps one little piece of information that still needs to be found. You need to solve the mysteries right away, but after you know what's here, the clues that you find in the Library will make far more sense.

📖 What does the Marker Switch at the far end of the pier do? Perhaps it controls something on another part of the Island.

The Myst Library

The Library is the focal point of Myst Island. You'll find yourself spending a lot of time here absorbing the information contained in the Library's many books.

The Library contains a wealth of information and hints that will become valuable in your quest to uncover the mystery of Myst. It is highly recommended that you take the time to examine the materials inside the Library before setting out to explore, because doing so will make your effort much more productive. It will also help you to make important connections as to how and where hints can be used.

Upon entering the Library, you'll see that it is filled with lots of valuable resources. Each wall inside the Library includes a special feature. Moving clockwise from left to right, those features are: a Map, a Red Book, a Painting, a Bookshelf, another Painting, a Blue Book, and a Fireplace.

📖 The map seems to be of Myst Island, but interestingly enough, there are no landmarks.

📖 On the pedestal lies a Red Book and a Red Page.

📖 If you return the page to the book, an interesting event occurs. Through heavy static, a man named Sirrus pleads you to help him escape from the book. It seems that he has been trapped and his only way out is to have the missing Red Pages returned to its book. But where can the Pages be found?

📖 The painting on the wall is quite odd. It appears to be a portrait of the Library with the front doors closed. What could that signify?

📖 There appears to be extensive damage to the Bookshelf collection. What could have happened here?

📖 If you take the time to search through the shelves, you'll find that a few of the volumes remain completely intact. Read carefully and you may learn something.

📖 This painting is almost a perfect match of the other, except that in this painting the Library doors are open. Could there be a connection between the two?

📖 Placing the Blue Page in the Blue Book produces a similar result as the Red Book, except that the person inside this book is a man named Achenar. Could it be your destiny to play savior to these two men?

The Myst Tower

While standing in the Pillar Walkway and facing the Library, you'll notice a large Tower extending from the rear of the Myst Library. Could this Tower be related to Atrus' message?

📖 The Tower provides a great view of Myst Island, but your first visit to the Library didn't seem to reveal an entrance—or did it?

📖 Can you put your finger on any-thing strange about this map?

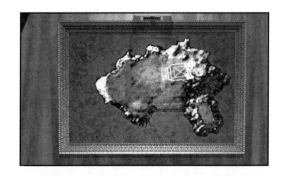

📖 Touching the Map reveals impor-tant clues. If you activated any of the Marker Switches on Myst Island, the landmarks near the switches will also be highlighted.

📖 When you move the pointing hand to the Tower landmark, a gripped hand appears. Follow the hand and see where it leads.

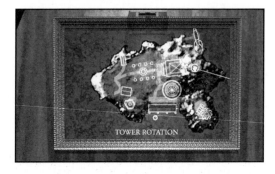

📖 The red lines on the map must indicate something. Did you notice the text and strange sound?

📖 Apparently the Map is some sort of control panel that rotates the Tower. When you feel comfort-able with the controls, the next order of business is to find the way up.

📖 Remember the twin-like pictures in the Library? Put your investigative skills to work to uncover the connection.

📖 After you find the entrance to the hallway, follow the path to an elevator.

📖 After you exit the elevator, scan the area thoroughly. Does the ladder behind the elevator lead to anything?

📖 The ladder leads to a view of the island, but what could the symbol underneath it mean? Wasn't there also a symbol by the other ladder?

📖 If you've properly learned to control the Tower Rotation device on the map, the ladders should lead to important clues. If not, you need to go back and try again.

📖 Try some different views. Besides the view itself, does anything else seem different when you rotate the Tower?

Operating the Dimensional Imager

The Dimensional Imager is located behind the doorway that leads off the pier.

- What happens when you touch the large button on the front of the Dimensional Imager?

- Are there any instructions located in the room?

- What happens when you touch the nail that holds the instruction sheet to the wall?

- Do the numbers written on the instruction sheet have any effect on the Dimensional Imager display?

- Have you seen or read anything that refers to the Dimensional Imager?

- Did Atrus' note hint at a number that could be entered into the control panel?

- How many Marker Switches are on Myst Island? Did you remember to count the Marker Switch next to the Clocktower?

For the Solution to this mystery, turn to page **28**.

The Sunken Gear

At the top of the hill, visible when you first enter Myst, are two large gears.

- There is another Marker Switch like the one on the pier. Does this switch control anything?

Operating the Planetarium

The Planetarium, a small domed building, sits just above the pier along the path that leads to the center of the island.

📖 Does the Marker Switch outside the Planetarium operate anything?

📖 What does the room look like when the lights are off?

📖 What do the controls above the chair do?

For the Solution to this mystery, turn to page **31**.

The Rocketship

The Rocketship, just past the Library on a causeway, looks ready to take off and carry you to unknown lands.

📖 Does the Marker Switch next to the ship do anything?

📖 Can you open the door to the Rocketship?

📖 Where does the power cable lead?

---

*For the Solution to this mystery, turn to page **32**.*

The Pillar Walkway

Located in front of the Library is a walkway surrounded by tall pillars.

📖 What happens when you move the pointer over one of the figures mounted in front of the pillars?

📖 What occurs when you press one of the figures?

📖 Does the model ship in the fountain remind you of anything?

📖 Does the Marker Switch at the end of the row of pillars do anything?

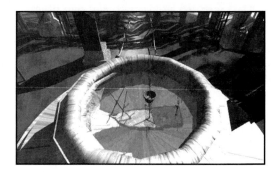

---

*For the Solution to this mystery, turn to page **32**.*

Operating the Generator

Past the Pillar Walkway is a small building.

- What is behind the door at the bottom of the staircase?

- Is there anything in the room that can help you decipher the controls?

- What happens when you press too many switches?

- Have you ever lost power to a room in your home? How did you fix this problem?

- How can you get to the top of the transmission pole?

- Where does the power line lead?

For the Solution to this mystery, turn to page 33.

The Log Cabin

Follow the path from the Clocktower to the small Log Cabin.

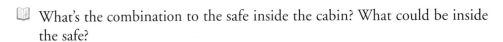

- 📖 There's another Marker Switch. What does this one do?

- 📖 What happens when you turn the handle next to the boiler?

- 📖 Is the pilot light under the boiler lit?

- 📖 What's the combination to the safe inside the cabin? What could be inside the safe?

- 📖 What's behind the Log Cabin?

- 📖 Do you hear anything when you turn the handle? Follow the sound. What do you see?

- 📖 What's the connection between the Log Cabin and the Giant Tree?

*For the Solution to this mystery, turn to page **35**.*

Operating the Clocktower

At the end of the path, past the Generator building, is a small island with a Clocktower.

- What time does the Clocktower read? Does the time ever change?

- What do the two handles located on the shore across from the Clocktower do? Do the handles perform exactly the same thing?

- What does the red button do?

- Can you reach the Marker Switch next to the Clocktower?

For the Solution to this mystery, turn to page **35**.

The Solutions

You find yourself alone on a small, bizarre island. There is no one to ask questions, no one to give you answers. What clues are there on this island that can help you solve the mystery of how you got here and, more important, how you can return home?

To understand Myst, your best bet is to walk around the entire island. Strictly speaking, there is only one solution for this section: How to work the Dimensional Imager. The rest of this section provides you with instructions on how each mechanism works (if it can be made to work at this time) and what to look for in each area. The clues that you obtain later in the game will make far more sense if you have a good working knowledge of Myst Island.

From your starting point, you can see a small hill with a couple of giant gears jutting from it. To your left is a small door and two buildings.

On your right, just peering above the waves, is the crow's nest of a Sunken Ship.

- Walk toward the pedestal at the end of the pier. Flip up the switch.

The Myst Library

- There are four books on the bookshelf that contain vital information. Each relates the story of Atrus and his visits to a particular Age and offers important clues. The information is summarized as follows:

BOOK LOCATION	COLOR	AGE	CLUES
Top Center	Green	Channelwood	Location of door lever
Top Right	Gray	Stoneship	Constellations
Center Left	Blue	Selenitic	Organ notes
Bottom Left	Brown	Mechanical	Tower Rotation Simulator

- Achenar and Sirrus, the men trapped in the books, are the sons of Atrus. At this point, how and why they have been trapped is unclear. In your travels, you must find missing pages that need to be returned to the books. Each returned page helps clear up the static and leads you in your quest for the truth.

- From the Library, head to Atrus' Fore-Chamber, which can be accessed through the door by the Dock.

The Tower

📖 The Tower is a means of identifying the locations of the four books, which serve as entrances to the various Ages of Myst Island.

📖 To rotate the Tower you must touch the map, which creates an outline of the Library and the Tower. If you've turned on any of the Marker Switches located on the island, those landmarks will appear as well.

📖 Move the hand cursor to the Tower icon and you can rotate the direction it faces. A red line appears if the Tower is rotated to face a landmark of special significance.

📖 Leave the red line on one of these landmarks before heading up to the Tower.

📖 The paintings on the wall are the means of reaching the Tower. When you touch the "closed door painting," the image begins to swirl and a panel behind the bookshelf opens.

📖 At the end of the hallway, take the elevator up to the Tower. When you get out, the Book Ladder is directly in front of you.

📖 The Book symbol indicates that the view shows where the Book to an Age is located. The view is not really as important, because the Map should give the obvious location of the Book.

📖 If your view is that of a stone wall, it means that the Tower has not been aligned properly on the Map.

📖 Each time the Tower is rotated to a red line location on the map, search behind the elevator to find a Key Ladder. At the top, a Key

Plaque displays a different piece of data for the location. This is the Key information which must be utilized to open a gateway at the particular location.

📖 The Key information must be used at a different landmark, which in turn activates the ability to access the Book location.

For example, the **2:40/2,2,1** clue would be used at a separate landmark to find the Book hidden in the Giant Gears.

BOOK LOCATION	KEY INFORMATION
Giant Gears	2:40/2,2,1
Giant Tree	7,2,4
Spaceship	59 Volts
Sunken Ship	October 11, 1984; 10:04 AM January 17, 1207; 5:46 AM November 23, 9791; 6:57 PM

Operating the Dimensional Imager

The Dimensional Imager, located at the bottom of the passageway off the pier, displays only some pretty, but unhelpful, 3-D pictures… or does it?

📖 Touch the small green switch located in the upper left-hand corner of the sheet of paper opposite the imager. Doing so reveals a control panel.

📖 Enter **08** (for the number of Marker Switches you found) into the controller and push the green button at the bottom of the imager. Now turn around and push the large button on the front of the imager.

📖 A message from Atrus tells you that the Library and the books it contains are very important. You also learn that one or both of Atrus' sons, Achenar and Sirrus, is behind the destruction of some of his books. There is also a Tower of Rotation that can be used instead of the books Atrus has hidden… but for what?

📖 Go to the Library.

📖 There are two books in the Library—one Red and one Blue—that have pieces of paper lying next to them. Pick up each piece of paper and insert it into the book lying next to the paper.

📖 Touch the cover of each book to open them and listen to the messages from Achenar and Sirrus.

The Sunken Gear

📖 Continue up the stairs. Turn right and climb up to the big gears. Flip up the switch there as well.

📖 Head back down the hill and across the ledge over the pier. Turn up the stairs and head toward the two buildings. The first building is the Planetarium and the second is the Library.

📖 Pick up the piece of paper lying on the ground on your way to the Planetarium.

📖 Written on the paper is a message from Atrus to his wife, Catherine, that tells how to use the Dimensional Imager located in the Fore-Chamber beside the dock. The Fore-Chamber is located behind the door on the pier. After you have counted all of the Marker Switches (on the pedestals that you have been flipping up), return to the pier to use the imager.

📖 The Sunken Gear prepares you for the Mechanical Age.

Operating the Planetarium

The Planetarium is small and seats only one person at a time in the control chair. In front of the Planetarium is another Marker Switch. Flip up the switch.

📖 Turn off the light switch next to the door and look up at the ceiling.

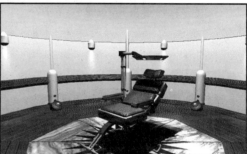

📖 Climb into the control seat and push the button in the middle of the control panel above your head. The sliders on the right side of the panel determine the date and time, while the display shows a constellation based on that date. (Push the button in the middle of the panel to update the constellation.) You will receive clues later in the game that tell you exactly what to set the date to.

📖 The Planetarium helps you find the Stoneship Age.

The Rocketship

Past the Library is a causeway that leads out to a classic Buck Rogers-esque Rocketship. A power cable extends from the ship along the coast of the island.

- 📖 In front of the Rocketship is another Marker Switch. Flip up the switch.

- 📖 The Rocketship takes you to the Selenitic Age.

The Pillar Walkway

Outside the Library is a collection of tall pillars that line a well tended path. In the middle of the path is a small fountain.

- 📖 In front of each pillar is a small box with a figure on it. Press one of the figures and notice how it changes from red to green when you touch it. Remember that each figure was originally red.

- Submerged in the fountain is a model of a sailing ship that looks a lot like the one next to the pier. This group of pillars must have some connection to the ship.

- Another Marker Switch is located toward the end of the Pillar Walkway. Flip it up as well.

- The Pillar Walkway moves you one step closer to the Stoneship Age.

Operating the Generator

On the right-hand side of the path, just past the Pillar Walkway, is a small building with a Marker Switch outside. Flip up the Marker Switch.

- Inside the building, follow the staircase down to the generator room. After entering, turn around to see a small piece of paper that has brief instructions describing how to operate the generator.

- Pushing any of the buttons on the control panel causes the voltage (indicated on the dials) to increase. In different combinations, the voltage can reach many different levels. Notice that if the voltage gets too high, everything shuts off because you've popped a circuit breaker somewhere. (Before you fix the popped circuit, remember to shut off all of the power switches so you don't pop another circuit breaker.)

- There are no circuit breakers in the generator room, so they must be somewhere outside. Leave the generator building, turn left, and walk down the slope toward the coast.

There is a power cable that runs from the generator building. This is the same cable that leads to the Rocketship. Between the cables and the instructions in the generator room, you should realize that the generator is needed to activate the Rocketship.

Continue down until you reach a pole with a ladder set into its side. At the top you can see a circuit breaker switch.

Climb the ladder and check the switch. If it's pointing down, flip it up.

If you still can't get the generator to deliver any power, check the other circuit breaker pole that's off the causeway next to the Rocketship.

The Generator prepares you for entrance to the Selenitic Age.

Operating the Clocktower

At the end of the path from the Pillar Walkway is the Clocktower and a box with two handles. There is also a Marker Switch next to the Clocktower, but you can't get to it to turn it on.

- 📖 Reach down to the handles and rotate them. Note that the large handle controls the clock's hour hand while the small handle controls the minute hand.

- 📖 You can set the time but what good does it do? You will get a clue to the clock's operation later.

- 📖 The Clocktower is one clue that leads you nearer the Mechanical Age.

The Log Cabin

Turn left from the Clocktower and walk up the small path to the Log Cabin. Flip up the final Marker Switch.

Inside the Cabin is a large boiler, a valve handle, a painting of a big tree, and a safe.

Rotating the handle next to the boiler has no effect. But when you look more closely, you notice that the pilot light (the lower left-hand opening under the boiler) is out.

Without the proper combination, you can't open the safe.

Outside the cabin, turn left and head toward the big tree. Its height and the platform built around it make this tree seem extremely significant. Also notice that this is the same tree used as the basis of the painting in the Log Cabin.

The Log Cabin helps you gain entrance to the Channelwood Age.

Chapter 3
The Selenitic Age

"*Though this world has little visual excitement to offer, it offers much to the ears. Sounds constantly flow through my ears and I have found where a few of them originate. It seems (as Catherine says) I do find beauty in everything.*"

The Selenitic Age Journal
Atrus

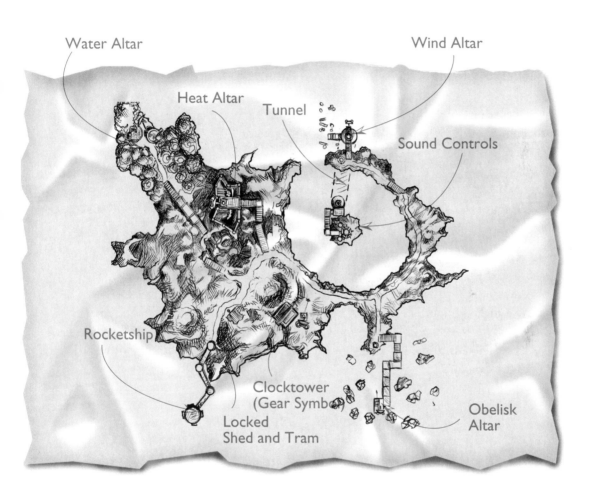

Water Altar

Heat Altar

Tunnel

Wind Altar

Sound Controls

Rocketship

Clocktower
(Gear Symbol)

Locked
Shed and Tram

Obelisk
Altar

The History of the Selenitic Age

At one point in time the Selenitic Age was a sprawling land of green hills. However, this all changed when a great meteor shower spewed fire and scorched the land. Although the lake was destroyed by the heat, a large cavity was opened in the land by the volcano debris which tapped into and created a larger body of water. Atrus also discovered two more things in his journey. First, the heat from the chasm in the ground could be manipulated and used as a powerful source of energy. Second, a vast tunnel system stretched beneath the land. Ironically, this is the only land in which Atrus did not find inhabitants.

A Guided Tour

As you explore the Selenitic Age, you'll notice that this world has the most solid ground on which to travel. Following the path from the Rocketship, you first come across a locked brick shed. From here, you can follow the path in any of three directions, which eventually lead you to one of the five altars. Although all of the altars are fairly standard in design, there are two unique features you'll discover at each landmark. The first is a gold plate with a different symbol at each location, while the second is the distinct sound of the area. Beyond these items, the only other significant landmark of interest is a small island with machinery located just offshore.

The Hints

Atrus describes the Selenitic Age as having been quite lush and beautiful before a great catastrophe turned it into a barren wasteland. Despite its sandy expanses, it is still an Age filled with awe inspiring vistas and challenging puzzles.

Entering the Selenitic Age from Myst Island

Where is the clue to entering the Selenitic Age from Myst Island? What steps must you take to use this clue?

📖 What is the link between the generator and the Rocketship?

📖 Have you turned on the Marker Switch in front of the Rocketship? What effect does this have on the map in the Library?

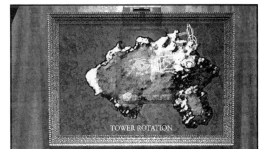

📖 When the tower rotation line on the map in the Library is pointed at the Rocketship marker and turns red, what is found at the top of the Key ladder in the observatory? What do you see out the window at the top of the Book ladder?

📖 What device or location lets you specify a voltage?

📖 Do all of the buttons on the generator control panel cause the same change in voltage?

📖 What combination of buttons adds up to **59** volts?

📖 If you go over **59** volts, what happens to the Rocketship voltage gauge?

- 📖 Have you ever lost power in one room of your house? How did you fix it?

- 📖 Where might a circuit breaker be located?

- 📖 How can you get to the top of the transmission pole?

- 📖 Might there be another circuit breaker pole closer to the Rocketship?

- 📖 Does correctly setting the voltage in the generator have any effect on the Rocketship?

- 📖 What is inside the Rocketship?

- 📖 What do the sliders on the control panel do?

- 📖 Have you seen an organ keyboard anywhere else?

- 📖 What tune did the Selenitic Age Journal have written in it?

- 📖 Could the tune have something to do with the control panel?

For the Solution to this mystery, turn to page 47.

Activating the Main Antenna

You see an odd-looking island upon entering the Selenitic Age. Does the technology-covered island in the middle of the lagoon have some special significance?

- 📖 Can you open the door at the end of the causeway?

- Again, another control panel? What combination must be entered to open this lock? What are the five sounds the panel makes?

- What is at the end of the path leading up from the stairway?

- Does the symbol mean anything?

- What happens to the symbol when you push the button directly under it?

- What sound do you hear at the Chasm?

- Is there something down the path that forks away from the locked door?

- What is on the bench next to the control panel?

- What happens if you push the button under the symbol? What is the symbol?

- What sound do you hear at the Oasis?

- Is there anything along the path that follows the edge of the lagoon?

- What happens if you push the button under the Clocktower symbol? What is the Clocktower symbol?

- What sound do you hear at the Clocktower?

- Does the lagoon path continue past the Clocktower?

Is there anything out on the dock in the Stone Forest? What is the Stone Forest symbol?

What happens if you pick up one page when you're already holding another?

What happens if you push the button on the control panel?

What do you find if you keep following the lagoon path?

Does anything happen if you push the button under the Wind Tunnel symbol? What is the Wind Tunnel symbol?

Where does the tunnel under the Wind Tunnel control panel go?

What happens if you touch the Main Antenna base?

Have you seen the symbols on the control panel before?

What happens if you point the Main Antenna at one of the other antenna locations on the island?

Can the Main Antenna be tuned so there is no static when you tune in to a particular location?

Does it matter what location you point the Main Antenna to when a certain symbol is highlighted on the control panel?

What happens if you enter all of the locations into the control panel?

Does the "sigma" button on the bottom of the control panel do anything?

For the Solution to this mystery, turn to page **51**.

Entering the Maze

Traveling the Maze brings you closer to the end of your journey in the Selenitic Age.

Does the sequence of five sounds from the Main Antenna have any significance?

Where have you heard these five sounds all in one place before?

What happens if you enter the five sounds, in order, into the control panel next to the locked door?

Where does the passageway lead?

What is inside the Mazerunner?

How do you control the Mazerunner?

Do certain sounds relate to a particular direction? What does it mean if you don't hear a sound?

Do the sounds you hear when the Mazerunner stops mean anything? Is there a pattern to the sounds? What does it mean when two of the sounds play at the same time?

If you take a wrong turn in the Mazerunner, how can you get back to your last correct location?

For the Solution to this mystery, turn to page 57.

Returning the Pages to Myst Island

At the end of the Maze, you must find your way to the Myst book so you can return the pages to the Myst Island Library.

How do you know you are at the end of the Maze? Can you turn the Mazerunner? Is there anything different about the walls of the Maze?

Is there anything outside the Mazerunner?

For the Solution to this mystery, turn to page 59.

The Solutions

The Rocketship, docked at the end of a high causeway next to the Myst Library, is especially enticing. The *art deco* craft promises trips to far off lands with strange landscapes. It does not fail in its promise.

Entering the Selenitic Age from Myst Island

Entering the Selenitic Age is not as simple as hopping in the Rocketship and flipping on the hyperdrive switch. That would be too easy. First you must find the clue that lets you open the ship and then figure out how to start the ship.

Start looking for your clues in the Library in the Myst Island painting.

📖 Open the Selenitic Age Journal on the bookshelves in the Library. At the back of this book is a picture of a piano keyboard with some of the keys highlighted. Note the highlighted keys and their order.

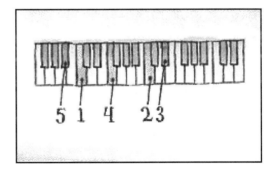

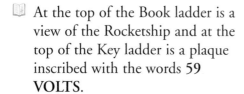 Rotate the tower to the Rocketship's position.

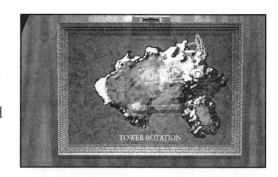 Go to the Observatory at the top of the Tower. If you haven't already been there, you must find the secret passage leading to it.

 At the top of the Book ladder is a view of the Rocketship and at the top of the Key ladder is a plaque inscribed with the words **59 VOLTS**.

📖 Leave the Tower and Library (open the door to the Library using the Open Door Painting) and walk to the generator building.

📖 Go down to the control room and set the generators to produce **59** volts by pushing the buttons as shown in the figure (buttons **1** and **3** in the left-hand column and buttons **3** and **4** in the right-hand column).

📖 If you push the wrong button and the right-hand voltage meter drops to zero, you have popped a circuit breaker. Turn off the generators and climb the two circuit breaker poles (along the power cable to the Rocketship) and reset the switches mounted on them. Then set the voltage again.

📖 After the voltage has been properly set, go to the Rocketship and push the door to open it.

Inside the Rocketship you find a control panel and an organ straight out of *20,000 Leagues Under the Sea.* Play the tune shown in the Selenitic Age Journal.

Move the five sliders on the control panel to duplicate the notes you played on the organ. (If you have trouble matching the notes, count the number of keys, including sharps and flats from the left-hand side of the keyboard and move the sliders up that many notes.)

Pull the handle on the right side of the control panel and a book floats in the vision screen in front of you. Touch the screen and the view changes to a fly-over of a small island.

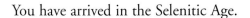 Touch the screen again and everything goes blank for a moment and you're still exactly where you started. Or are you? Turn around. The view out of the open hatchway has changed.

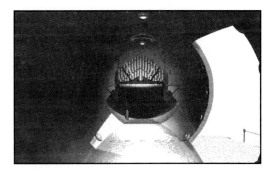

You have arrived in the Selenitic Age.

Activating the Main Antenna

The main antenna, mounted on an island in the middle of the lagoon, provides the clue needed to get to the next step in the Selenitic Age.

 Walk along the causeway to the island. Pass by the doorway on your right, you need the main antenna clue to open it.

 Proceed to a stairway on your left. Follow the stairway and the path beyond it to a small control panel located above a flaming Chasm.

Note the symbol on the control panel and the noise you hear. Push the button to light up the symbol.

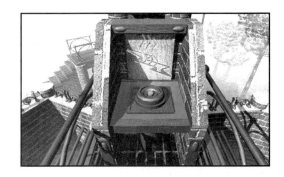

Leave the Chasm and walk to the end of the stairs. Follow the right-hand path, leading away from the locked doorway.

Follow the path to the Oasis, the one place on this island that has vegetation.

At the top of the hill you will find another control panel and a bench with a Blue page. Take the page.

Listen to the sound and note the symbol on the control panel. Push the button on the panel to illuminate the symbol.

Return to the fork in the path and walk along the water to the Clocktower.

Note the sound that the clock makes and the symbol on its control panel. Push the control panel button.

Continue along the path to a right-hand turn.

Walk out to the pier in the Stone Forest. On it you will find another control panel and a Red page. If you've already taken the Blue page, you must return it to the Library before you can pick up the Red page.

Listen to the sound of the Stone Forest and note the symbol on the control panel. Push the button on the panel.

Head back to the path and continue around the lagoon to the Wind Tunnel opening.

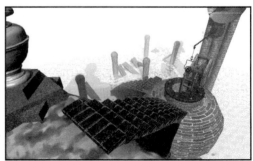

Note the sound of the Wind Tunnel and its symbol. Push the control panel button.

Climb down the ladder into the Wind Tunnel. Turn on the light switch at the bottom.

Follow the Wind Tunnel and climb the ladder at the other end.

At the top of the ladder is the Main Antenna. Inside the mounting is another, more sophisticated control panel.

Touch the mounting to open the control panel.

For each of the five buttons along the bottom, use the rotation buttons to point the antenna at the appropriate location. When the antenna is set right, you will hear the noise from that location, without any static. Push the next location button and set the angle for it. Use the following figures as references for the proper angles.

When each of the location angles has been properly set, push the "sigma" button at the bottom of the other control panel. The sounds for each location will play in a specific order. Note the order.

Entering the Maze

Return to the locked door at the other end of the island. Move each of the sliders so that they play the noises from the five locations in the order you heard at the Main Antenna (Oasis, Chasm, Clocktower, Stone Forest, Wind Tunnel).

Push the red button on the right of the control panel to open the door.

📖 Pass through the door and follow it to the Mazerunner.

📖 Open the door to the Mazerunner and climb inside.

📖 Get into the chair and press the Forward button. The Maze-runner descends deep under the island to a maze of railroad tracks. Each time you push the Forward button from now on, the Mazerunner will move forward along the tracks. Each time it stops, you must decide on a

direction to point the Mazerunner based on the noise you hear. To set the direction, push one of the arrow buttons and watch the compass on the right of the control panel.

If you happen to make a wrong turn in the maze, push the Backtrack button to return you to your last correct location and listen to the noise again. If you need to repeat a noise, push the button mounted in the middle of the speaker.

There are four sounds corresponding to north, south, east, and west. If two sounds occur at the same time, say north and west, then the direction would be northwest. The four noises are:

North—Ping
South—Twang
East—Whoosh
West—Chirp

📖 To get through the Maze, start by going north. Then at each subsequent intersection, turn the following directions:

W, N, E, E, S, S, W, SW, W, NW, NE, N, SE

Returning the Pages to Myst Island

After finding the pages, you need to return them to the Myst Island Library.

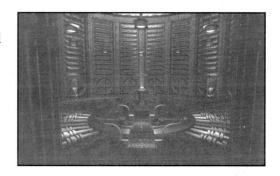

- 📖 At the end of the maze, push the blue button to open the door and exit to the corridor.

- 📖 Follow the corridor to the chamber containing a book.

- 📖 Open the book and touch the swirling image of the Library ceiling. You are transported back to the Library.

- 📖 Place the appropriate page in the correct brother's book to complete the Selenitic Age.

Chapter 4
The Stoneship Age

"*Even though the boat cannot move, I have enjoyed studying from it... I now have answers to a few of the questions my father never answered.*"

The Stoneship Age Journal
Atrus

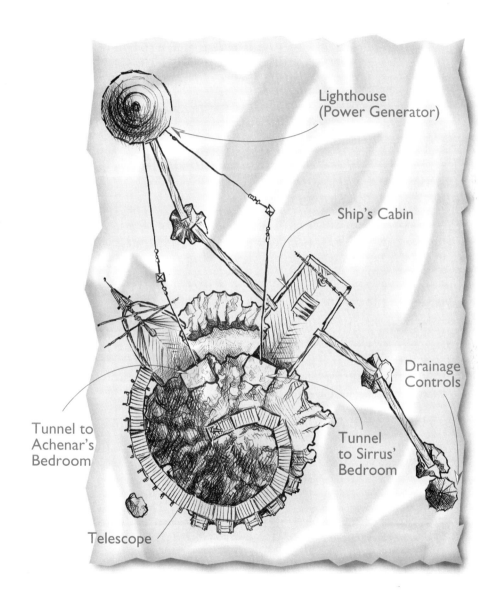

Lighthouse
(Power Generator)

Ship's Cabin

Drainage
Controls

Tunnel to
Achenar's
Bedroom

Tunnel
to Sirrus'
Bedroom

Telescope

The History of the Stoneship Age

The Stoneship Age is a magical land, as Atrus discovered with disastrous results. When writing in his journal about a ship, a boat materialized out of thin air, but was cut into two sections that were attached to the land. When he first arrived, Atrus shared the island with only three young boys, and in hopes of drawing attention to the island, he constructed a great lighthouse that would serve as a beacon to others who might be near. It worked quite well, because the population increased by a remarkable number in a short period of time. When Atrus returned a number of years later, he found the land had begun to sink and the people gone.

A Guided Tour

You begin the Stoneship Age on the back half of a ship that has been fused into the large, rocky piece of land. The tunnel cut into the rock and the below-deck cabin seem to be inaccessible because they are flooded with water. Three paths extend from the starting point. In one direction, a single path leads out to a control panel that is covered by an umbrella. In the other direction are two paths. One leads to the Lighthouse, which not surprisingly is also flooded, while the path along the rocks leads to the front half of the ship. There is also a flooded tunnel entrance at this location. Continuing along the rocky path, you'll find a telescope that overlooks the island.

The Hints

Traveling through the Stoneship Age is a mighty task. Is it possible to raise a sunken ship from the depths of the sea? Some of the mysteries may be solved by discovering how Sirrus and Achenar live their lives.

Entering the Stoneship Age from Myst Island

What is the clue on Myst Island that leads you to the Stoneship Age?

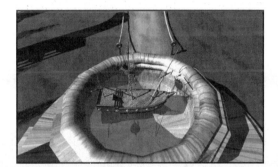

- What is the link between the Sunken Ship at the dock and the model ship in the fountain?

- Have you turned on the Marker Switch on the dock? Does this have an effect on the map in the Library?

- When the Tower Rotation line on the map in the Library is pointed at the dock, what can you find at the top of the ladders in the Observatory?

- Is there an object or place on the island that is designed for you to enter dates and times?

- What do the constellations in the Planetarium mean?

- Where would you find a reference about constellations?

- Do the patterns shown under the constellations in the Stoneship Age journal occur anywhere else on the island?

For the Solution to this mystery, turn to page 67.

It's now time to explore the Stoneship Age.

Activating the Generator

The two tunnels under the island are quite dark. How can you supply electricity to the lights?

- Where do the cables from the two tunnels lead?

- Is there anything inside the Lighthouse? How can you unlock the door at the top of the ladder?

- What do the three switches at the end of the dock do?

- How can you drain the water from the flooded Lighthouse?

- Is there anything in the basement of the Lighthouse?

- Does the valve serve a purpose?

- Can you lift or open the trunk?

- What is inside the trunk?

For the Solution to this mystery, turn to page 71.

Finding the Red and Blue Pages

Your goal is to find the Red and Blue pages and return them to Sirrus' and Achenar's books in the Myst Library.

- What lights are turned on after you charge the batteries in the generator room?

- How can you pump the water out of the tunnels?

- What is at the bottom of the tunnels?

- Is there anything important— besides the Blue page—in Achenar's bedroom?

For the Solution to this mystery, turn to page 74.

Returning the Pages to Myst Island

After you have found the Blue and Red pages, you must return them to the appropriate book in the Library on Myst Island.

- Is there something at the top of the spiral staircase near the walkway?

- What can you see through the telescope?

- The telescope indicates the blinking light is coming from what direction?

- Are the doors to the bedrooms the only exits from the tunnels under the island?

- What do the buttons on the compass rose do?

- What is at the bottom of the staircase at the stern of the ship?

For the Solution to this mystery, turn to page 76.

The Solutions

Stoneship. It's an odd name that brings to mind images of boats too heavy to float. The reality is even stranger than that.

Entering the Stoneship Age from Myst Island

The Sunken Ship at the dock and the model in the fountain are obviously connected. Figuring out the connection and dealing with the clues you find in the Library is your first task in this Age.

📖 Rotate the tower to the Sunken Ship off the dock. (Have you turned on its Marker Switch?)

📖 Go to the Observatory at the top of the tower. If you haven't already been there, you will need to find the secret passage that leads to it.

At the top of the Book ladder is a view of the Sunken Ship, while at the top of the Key ladder is a plaque inscribed with three dates and times.

Leave the tower and the Library and walk to the Planetarium.

Turn off the lights in the Planetarium, and then climb into the chair in the middle of the room.

Enter the dates and times into the control panel above the chair and push the large start button. The display shows a constellation for each date. Mark down the three constellations.

📖 Return to the Library and remove the Stoneship Age journal from the shelves.

Flip to the back of the book and look up the three constellations, noting the figures drawn under them.

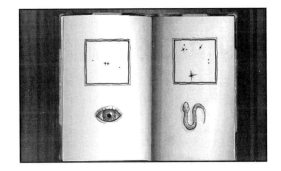

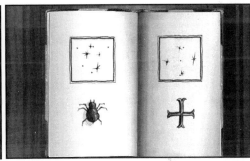

📖 Go to the Pillar Walkway and touch the three pillars that correspond to the three figures you found in the book. Make sure each of the figures turns green. If you've previously touched any of the other symbols, make sure they are now red. When the three correct pillar symbols are green,

you hear a "gurgling" noise and when you look in the fountain, all of the water has drained out of it, leaving the model high and dry. In addition, the ship off the dock has been raised.

Go to the Sunken Ship off of the dock and climb aboard.

Enter the cabin in the stern of the ship. Take the book, open it, and touch the view of the Stoneship Age.

You are transported to the deck of a new ship: the Stoneship.

Activating the Generator

Before you can descend into the tunnels beneath the island, you must provide electricity for the lights. Because power cables extend from the two tunnel entrances and lead to the Lighthouse, this must indicate the generator's location.

Enter the Lighthouse. The way up to the generator room is locked and the basement is flooded. One key is attached to the floor with a chain that is far too short to reach the hatch.

📖 Go to the small umbrella-covered control panel and push the far right-hand button. A pumping sound starts and then stops.

📖 Return to the Lighthouse and walk down the stairs to the basement.

📖 Turn the valve on the trunk and let all of the water drain out. Don't forget to close the valve.

📖 Go back to the pump control panel and push the lighted, right-most button. The pumping sound resumes.

📖 Return to the Lighthouse and you'll see the trunk floating next to the key.

If the trunk isn't there, you forgot to close the valve before flooding the basement. Pump the water out of the basement again, close the valve on the trunk, and reflood the basement to float the trunk.

Grab the key on the deck and use it to open the trunk. Inside the trunk is another key.

Take this key and push the lock on the hatch to open it. The key will drop away.

Climb the ladder into the generator room. Inside you find a hand generator and storage batteries.

Crank the generator until the meter on the batteries is completely white, which indicates that they're fully charged. The charge lasts for about 10 minutes, after which time you must recharge the batteries.

Finding the Red and Blue Pages

Now that the lights in the tunnels have been turned on, it's time to start looking for Achenar's and Sirrus' pages.

📖 Go to the pump control panel and push the middle button. This pumps out the subterranean tunnels.

To find Sirrus' Red page:

📖 Return to the ship and take the first tunnel down into the island. At the bottom of the tunnel is Sirrus' bedroom.

📖 Sirrus' Red page is in the bottom drawer of the dresser.

To find Achenar's Blue page:

📖 Walk down into the tunnel from the bow of the ship. At the bottom is Achenar's bedroom.

📖 The Blue page is lying on Achenar's unkempt bed.

In the next-to-bottom drawer of the map case is a torn slip of paper that becomes important later in the game. Take note of it.

Returning the Pages to Myst Island

After you have found the Red and Blue pages, you must return them to their respective books in the Myst Library.

Climb the spiral staircase leading up from the bow of the ship. At the top of the staircase is a telescope.

Look through the telescope and drag the view to the right until you can see the top of the Lighthouse. If the battery is charged, you'll see a blinking red light on top that you can't see from ground level. The compass at the top of the telescope view indicates that the Lighthouse is at exactly **135** degrees.

Return to a tunnel that leads down to one of the bedrooms. On the first landing above each bedroom is a secret door.

Enter the secret passage and walk until you come to a compass rose.

Push the button on the compass rose that corresponds to **135** degrees (the angle taken from the telescope).

A light turns on outside of the windows.

📖 Return to the surface and walk out to the pump control panel.

📖 Push the left-most button on the control panel to pump out the water in the stern of the ship.

📖 Walk down the staircase and enter the room behind the door.

- Continue to walk down the stairs until you come to a table. Touch the table to make the Myst book materialize.

- Open the Myst book and touch the picture to return to the Library.

- Place the Blue and Red pages in their respective books.

Chapter 5
The Mechanical Age

"We have finally fin-
ished the fortress. It
rests between the
three hills which are
now only islands due to the rising
water level..."

The Mechanical Age Journal
Atrus

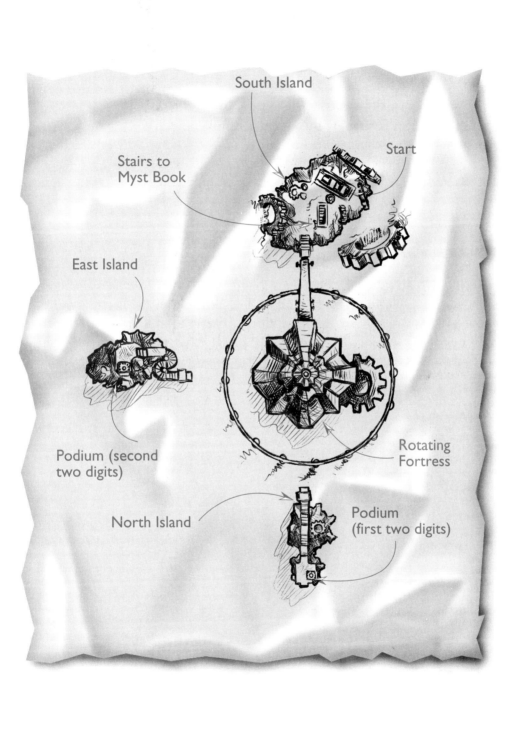

South Island

Start

Stairs to
Myst Book

East Island

Rotating
Fortress

Podium (second
two digits)

North Island

Podium
(first two digits)

The History of the Mechanical Age

When Atrus first ventured into the Mechanical Age, he found a desolated population isolated on a small group of rocks. It seems that a vicious band of invaders were responsible for destroying this once beautiful and peaceful community. To help ensure that this would never happen again, Atrus helped the inhabitants construct a vast Fortress in the center of the remaining points of land. Fortunately, when the invaders returned, the inhabitants were able to repel the invaders once and for all.

A Guided Tour

You begin your adventure on the South Island. From here, a bridge stretches to a cylindrical, metal Fortress in the center of the land. Within the Fortress, you'll find the living quarters of Achenar and Sirrus, as well as an inoperable elevator. Offshore to the North and East are islands similar to the South; however, there's one key difference: No bridge links these islands to the Fortress.

The Hints

Because it is true that all of the Myst Ages have machines in them, why should this one be singled out as the Mechanical Age?

Entering the Mechanical Age from Myst Island

What clue leads you to the Mechanical Age and where must you go first to use it?

📖 What is the largest obvious mechanical device on Myst Island?

📖 Have you turned on the Marker Switch in front of the Sunken Gear? What effect does this have on the map in the Library?

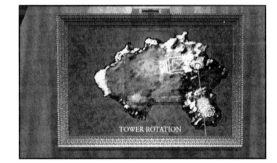

📖 When the Tower Rotation line on the map in the Library is pointed at the Sunken Gear marker, what do you see at the top of the two ladders in the Observatory?

📖 Is there anything on the island that's associated with time?

📖 How can you set the time on the Clocktower?

📖 What happens when you push the Red button under the clock control wheels *after* the clock has been set to **2:40**?

📖 What's inside the Clocktower?

📖 How can you change only one number?

📖 What happens if you hold down one of the levers?

*For the Solution to this mystery, turn to page **86**.*

Finding the Red and Blue Pages

To find Achenar's Blue page:

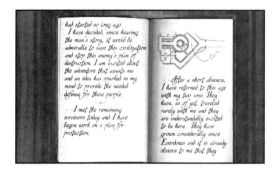

📖 Have you completely searched Achenar's bedroom?

📖 Does the drawing of the Fortress from the Mechanical Age journal show a room linked to Sirrus' bedroom? Might there be a similarly linked room off of Achenar's?

*For the Solution to this mystery, turn to page **90**.*

To find Sirrus' Red page:

📖 Have you searched Sirrus' room completely?

📖 Does the drawing of the Fortress from the Mechanical Age journal show a room linked to Sirrus' bedroom?

📖 Could something be covering part of the entrance to this room?

📖 Is there anything in any of the boxes piled up around the room?

*For the Solution to this mystery, turn to page **91**.*

Returning the Pages to Myst Island

After you have found the Blue and Red pages, you must return them to the appropriate book in the Library on Myst Island.

- What purpose does the Rotation Simulator with two control levers in Achenar's room serve?

- What could the sounds that the Rotation Simulator makes possibly mean?

- Is there anything in the corridor that links Sirrus' and Achenar's bedrooms?

- How can you open the elevator?

- What is at the bottom of the steps leading down from the corridor?

- What do the two c-shaped indicators mean? What happens when they are lined up?

- Do the three buttons in the elevator all do the same thing?

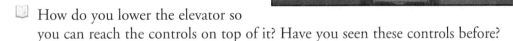

- What is at the top of the elevator car?

- Is there anything important in the room?

- How do you lower the elevator so you can reach the controls on top of it? Have you seen these controls before?

- Can you get out of the elevator before it starts moving?

- In what directions are the three islands arranged?

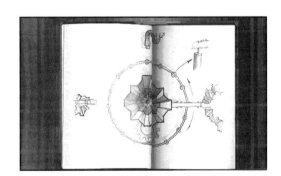

- What is on the two other islands?

- Have you seen a pedestal like these before?

For the Solution to this mystery, turn to page **92.**

The Solutions

Although all of the Myst Ages have machines of one sort or another, the Mechanical Age takes this concept to a new extreme. The entire Age is a machine that you must learn to operate in order to return to Myst.

Entering the Mechanical Age from Myst Island

The Sunken Gear above the pier is the obvious entrance to the Mechanical Age, but accessing the book that transports you there takes you on a journey over all of Myst Island.

- Rotate the Tower to the Sunken Gear. (Have you turned on its Marker Switch?)

- Go to the Observatory at the top of the Tower. If you haven't already been there, you need to find the secret passage that leads to it.

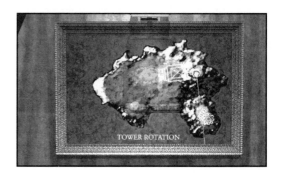

TOWER ROTATION

Through the window at the top of the Book ladder you can see the Sunken Gear, while the Key ladder has a plaque inscribed with a time and three numbers.

📖 Leave the Tower and Library and walk to the Clocktower.

📖 Set the time on the clock to **2:40** using the control wheels mounted on the shore. The large wheel sets the minutes (in five minute increments), while the small wheel sets the hour.

When the time has been set properly, push the Red button. A walkway made of gears rises out of the water.

Walk over the gear bridge to the Clocktower and enter the clock. (If you want, flip the Marker Switch on before entering the clock.)

Inside you find the clockwork mechanism with a three-number sequence of gears at its top.

Set the mechanism to **3,3,1** by doing the following: pull down the left handle to rotate the lower two numbers, and keep the handle pulled until the middle number rotates by itself.

Now pull and release the right handle twice to turn the upper two numbers so that the system reads **2,2,1** just like the clue in the Observatory.

The large gear at the bottom of the mechanism rotates halfway but reveals nothing inside; however, it does indicate that the actual gear by the dock has rotated.

📖 Walk to the Sunken Gear at the other end of the island and notice that it has rotated as well.

📖 Continue up to the Gear and take the book that has been uncovered. Touch the image inside to go to the Mechanical Age.

Finding the Red and Blue Pages

Your first objective in this new Age is to find the brothers' pages.

📖 Walk to the Fortress across the bridge.

To find Achenar's Blue page:

📖 Turn right upon entering the Fortress and walk to the end of the hallway. This is Achenar's bedroom.

📖 In his bedroom is a throne and next to it an indentation in the wall with a wide yellow stripe. Touch the stripe to reveal a secret room.

In the room you can find the Blue page on the bottom of a set of shelves.

To find Sirrus' Red page:

Turn left at the Fortress entrance and walk to Sirrus' bedroom.

Below and to the right of the throne is a small indentation in the wall that is partially obscured by an object on the wall. Touch the indentation to reveal the secret room.

📖 Sirrus' Red page is in the boxes in the far corner of the room. Just touch the cover of the box to reveal its contents.

Returning the Pages to Myst Island

Your task now is to return the pages to Sirrus' and Achenar's books on Myst Island.

📖 Go to Achenar's bedroom. Next to the throne and secret door is a Fortress Rotation Simulator. Touch the machine to activate it.

This imager projects a simulation of the Fortress and shows how it can be rotated to permit access to the three islands that surround it.

📖 Pull the left-hand lever to unlock the rotation mechanism. Now pull the right-hand lever and watch the line rotate. Notice that when you let go of the lever, the line swings back and forth and comes to rest at one of the four arrows. When you push the left-hand lever back into place, the machine makes one of four noises based on the direction in which it is pointed.

North—Ping
South—Twang
East—Whoosh
West—Chirp

At the back of Achenar's bedroom is another corridor that goes directly to Sirrus' bedroom. Halfway down the corridor is a turnoff that leads to what looks like an elevator.

Push the button next to the turnoff to reveal a set of steps leading down below the elevator.

Pull the lever on the control panel until the two c-shapes are aligned. This opens the elevator door.

Return to the top of the stairs and push the button again to raise the stairs back into place.

Enter the elevator and press the up arrow.

At the top is an empty room except for an elevator; although it is curious that there seem to be two control levers on top of the elevator car.

Get back into the elevator, push the middle button, and then step back out of the elevator. It drops by about half its length, providing easy access to the control panel on top of the car.

Use the two levers to direct the Fortress at the east island. Pull the left lever to release the Fortress and pull the right one to rotate it. You have reached the correct angle when you hear the "Whoosh" sound.

📖 Retrieve the elevator by pushing the small button between the two levers. Leave the Fortress and walk to the new island.

📖 At the top of the island you can find a pedestal like the one near the Sunken Gear where you first appeared in this Age. Note the two symbols on top of the pedestal and the fact that they are on the right-hand side.

📖 Return to the rotation controls on top of the elevator in the Fortress. Set the Fortress so that it points to the north island, which makes a "Ping" sound.

📖 Exit the Fortress again and walk to the north island.

There is another pedestal here with two more symbols. Note the two symbols and the fact that they are on the left-hand side.

Return once again to the rotation controls on the elevator. This time set the rotation so the Fortress faces the south island ("Twang" sound), which is where you entered this Age.

Walk to the pedestal next to the Sunken Gear.

Enter the four symbols you found on the two other islands and push the large button.

A set of stairs opens up next to the bridge to the Fortress.

Walk down the stairs to the Myst book. Push the image inside the book to return to the Library.

Insert the pages you retrieved into the correct books to complete the Mechanical Age.

Chapter 6
The Channelwood Age

"Water covers this age as far as I can see except for a small rocky island. Elsewhere, there are only trees that grow directly out of the water. A myriad of thin wooden passageways are built just above the water and disappear into the forest."

The Channelwood Age Journal
Atrus

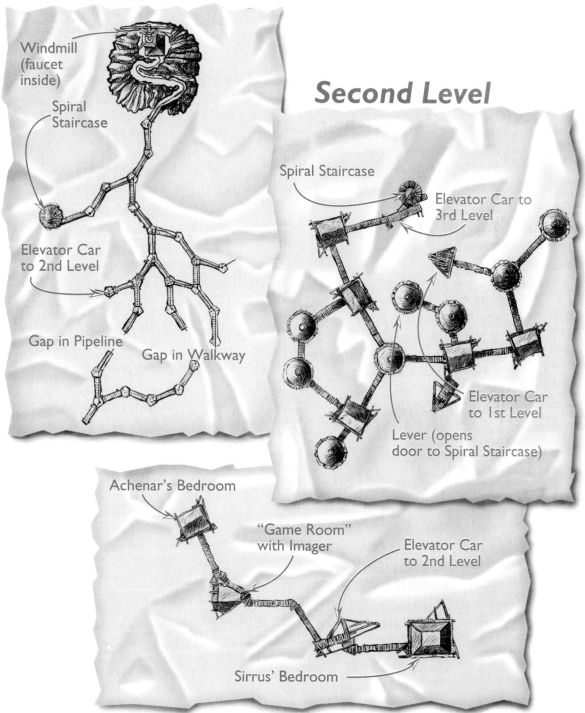

First Level

Windmill (faucet inside)

Spiral Staircase

Elevator Car to 2nd Level

Gap in Pipeline

Gap in Walkway

Second Level

Spiral Staircase

Elevator Car to 3rd Level

Elevator Car to 1st Level

Lever (opens door to Spiral Staircase)

Third Level

Achenar's Bedroom

"Game Room" with Imager

Elevator Car to 2nd Level

Sirrus' Bedroom

The History of the Channelwood Age

According to Atrus' journals, the Channelwood Age was once populated by two unique life forms: humans and a race of monkey-like creatures. The two lived together, with the humans inhabiting the ground and the tree-dwellers in the trees. Then a great flood ravaged the land and the humans were forced to take to the trees as well. When Atrus arrived, only one human remained and he was worshipped as a leader by the creatures. After the leader died, the creatures turned their loyalty and attention to Atrus and his sons, but the creatures feared Achenar and Sirrus because of a previous experience. Sirrus and Achenar once forced the monkeys to eat people food while Atrus visited the other Ages. The monkeys hated the food, so Sirrus and Achenar whipped them until Atrus returned.

A Guided Tour

The Channelwood Age is almost completely water-covered and has the appearance of a swamp. It is easy to see why there was a necessity for living in the trees. Other than the wooden path on which you arrive, the only solid ground is a small rocky island that serves as a base for a Windmill. The wooden path leads to a number of places including dead ends, an inoperable elevator, a locked door, and the Windmill. High above in the trees, a sophisticated network of walkways link the houses of the tree-dwellers.

The Hints

The challenge before you in the Channelwood Age lies in the fact that the Age is almost entirely covered by water. The key is finding the appropriate path to maneuver through this Age.

Entering the Channelwood Age from Myst Island

Where can you find the clue that lets you enter the Channelwood Age? How do you use it after you've found it?

📖 Can there be any link between the Giant Tree, the cabin at the tree's base, and the book in the Library describing the Channelwood Age?

📖 Have you turned on the Marker Switch in front of the cabin? Does this have an effect on the map in the Myst Library?

📖 When the Tower Rotation line on the map in the Library turns red when pointed at the cabin marker, what can you find at the top of the Key ladder in the tower? Can you see anything out of the window at the top of the Book ladder?

📖 Where in the cabin can three numbers be entered?

How can you light the boiler? Does the pressure gauge change? How can you turn up the gas?

What is the banging noise you hear each time the pressure drops in the boiler? What happens if you turn off the gas after the noise stops? Could the noise be coming from outside or behind the cabin?

For the Solution to this mystery, turn to page **108**.

The Channelwood Age is ready for your exploration.

Activating the Power System

How can you supply power to the numerous machines and elevators in this age?

Do any of the machines or elevators work?

What is connected to all of the machines in this Age that may indicate a power source?

What do you find when you follow the pipes back to their source?

The windmill is turning, but do you hear any water flowing through the pipes outside the building?

Do you hear water flowing through the pipes at the machine you want to operate? What could direct the water to that machine?

For the Solution to this mystery, turn to page **111**.

Reaching the First Level of Treehouses

How can you reach the levels of treehouses above you?

Can you open the door to the spiral staircase? How about the door to the elevator (the one that can be reached without raising the Sunken Bridge)?

Does the elevator have power? How can you get power to it?

For the Solution to this mystery, turn to page **112**.

Reaching the Second Level of Treehouses

How can you reach the second level of treehouses?

📖 Does the elevator next to the spiral staircase have any power?

📖 If you go back down to water level by using the elevator, how can you get back up to the first level of treehouses to use the other elevator if you supply it with power?

📖 What happens when you pull the lever in the first level of treehouses?

For the Solution to this mystery, turn to page 114.

Finding the Red and Blue Pages

Your goal is to find the Red and Blue pages and return them to Sirrus' and Achenar's books in the Myst Library.

To find Sirrus' Red page:

📖 Which of the three rooms on the second level of treehouses do you think might be Sirrus' bedroom?

📖 What could Sirrus be hiding in the drawers in his bedroom?

For the Solution to this mystery, turn to page **116**.

To find Achenar's Blue page:

📖 Does the video imager in Achenar's bedroom conceal anything important?

📖 What is in the last remaining room on the second level of treehouses?

For the Solution to this mystery, turn to page **117**.

Returning the Pages to Myst Island

After you've found the Red and Blue pages, you need to return them to Myst Island; but where is the book that takes you there?

📖 Have you completed a thorough search of the water level?

📖 What does the mechanism next to the break in the walkway do? How can you direct water to the mechanism to make it work?

- What is past the break in the waterway?

- Where does the pipe to the third elevator come from?

- What can you find to lift the fallen pipe to make a connection with the other side of the break?

For the Solution to this mystery, turn to page **118**.

The Solutions

Finding the clue that directs you to a new Age is only half the battle. After you have the clue, you must figure out where and how to use it.

Entering the Channelwood Age from Myst Island

As always, the Library is the place to start looking for clues to entering a new Age.

📖 Rotate the tower in the Myst Island painting so it points to the Giant Tree. (Have you turned on all the Marker Switches?)

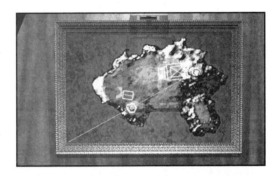

📖 Go to the room at the top of the Tower. If you haven't already been there, you need to find the access to the secret passage leading to it.

📖 At the top of the Book ladder is a view of the Giant Tree, and at the top of the Key ladder is a plaque with the numbers 7,2,4 etched into it.

📖 Leave the tower and Library (open the door to the Library using the Open Door Painting) and walk to the cabin under the Giant Tree.

In the cabin is a boiler, a big wheel, and a safe. There doesn't seem to be any flame under the boiler and the pressure gauge is at zero.

The safe has a three digit combination and contains a book of matches. Enter the three numbers (7,2,4) found in the Tower Rotation room to unlock the safe.

Touch the matchbox to open it, and then touch it again to remove a match. Drag the match and use it to start the pilot light under the boiler.

Rotate the wheel next to the boiler (when your cursor is green) to turn up the gas. Watch the pressure rise and then suddenly fall, accompanied by a loud banging noise.

When the noise stops, turn off the gas and leave the cabin. You'll notice that the noise starts again. After leaving the cabin, turn left and walk behind the cabin. From here you can see an elevator cut into the side of the tree. The elevator then drops downward.

Quickly go up to the platform and get into the elevator as it drops belowground. The elevator takes you to the Channelwood Age book room. (If you don't reach the elevator in time, go back to the cabin and turn up the gas to raise the elevator again.)

📖 Pick up the book and touch the image inside to be transported to the Channelwood Age.

The Channelwood Age is now ripe for exploring.

Activating the Power System

Looking around the Channelwood Age, it becomes clear that nothing is working. Providing power to the various machines will solve this problem.

📖 When you enter the Age, there is pipe at your feet. Follow the pipe back to the stone island with the windmill at its peak. Notice that all of the pipes converge into one pipe and finally lead off to this island.

In the building at the top of the island, turn on the valve so that water flows from the tank through the pipes scattered throughout the Channelwood Age.

When you want to operate a particular piece of machinery, you must set the valves to direct the flow so the water pressure reaches it. You may have to turn two or more valves, depending on which machine you want to use.

Reaching the First Level of Treehouses

Because there does not seem to be any Red or Blue pages on water level, it seems only logical to look for them in the treehouses that can be seen high overhead.

- Find the elevator closest to the spiral staircase.

- Provide power to the elevator by setting the valves in the pipes to direct water toward it.

- If you haven't already turned on the power at the windmill, do so now. If you need help, refer to the Solution section, "Activating the Power System."

- Enter the elevator, shut the door, and pull the lever to get to the first level of treehouses.

Reaching the Second Level of Treehouses

The first level of treehouses seems to contain only the ruins of some inhabitants' personal belongings, but no sign of Sirrus or Achenar. Better venture to the second level of treehouses.

📖 The Myst Library map, when activated, shows a treehouse with a dashed line extending to the stairway. Pull the lever in the treehouse and watch the door to the elevator swing open.

📖 Make your way to the elevator. Provide power to the elevator by setting the valves in the pipes to direct water toward it.

📖 Open the door to the stairway and walk down to the walkway level.

📖 Walk back up the stairs (the other elevator won't work now that you have activated this one) and enter the elevator. Shut the door and pull the lever to get to the second level of treehouses.

Finding the Red and Blue Pages

The second level of treehouses contains Achenar's and Sirrus' bedrooms, which are the standard places to find the missing pages.

To find Sirrus' Red page:

📖 After exiting the elevator on the second level of treehouses, turn left toward Sirrus' bedroom.

📖 Search all the drawers to find Sirrus' Red page and half of a piece of paper with a cryptic message scribbled on it.

📖 Return to Myst Island and put the page in Sirrus' book. Then return to the Channelwood Age for Achenar's Blue page.

To find Achenar's Blue page:

📖 After exiting the elevator, turn right and head past the "toy" room to Achenar's bedroom.

📖 Achenar's Blue page is lying on the floor next to an imager that displays messages from Achenar and Sirrus.

📖 Return to Myst Island to put the Blue page in Achenar's book.

Returning the Pages to Myst Island

After you have found the Blue and Red pages, you must return them to the appropriate book in the Library on Myst Island.

☐ Take the elevator down from the second level to the first level of treehouses. Then walk down the stairs to ground level.

☐ Find the gap in the walkway that has a cylindrical mechanism mounted next to it.

- Provide power to the mechanism by setting the valves in the pipes to direct water toward the gap.

- Pull the lever on the cylindrical mechanism to make the Sunken Bridge appear.

- Follow the walkway over the Sunken Bridge to the elevator. Note that there is a break in the power pipe at the other gap in the walkway.

Turn the handle next to the gap in the pipes to lift the pipe section into place.

Set the valves on the power pipes to direct water pressure to the elevator.

Enter the elevator, shut the door, and pull the lever to travel to the room containing the Myst book.

Open the Myst book and touch the picture to return to the Myst Island Library.

Place each page into its respective book to complete the Channelwood Age.

Chapter 7
D'ni, the End Game

"You've done the right thing. I have a difficult choice to make. My sons have betrayed me, I know what I must do."

D'ni, the End Game
Atrus

The Hints

The journey is nearly complete. Just a few more intricate puzzles to solve and the Myst mystery will be solved.

Entering the Fireplace

Both brothers tell you, after you give them the page from the final Age you've visited, that you must get one last page to free them.

📖 Remember to save your game.

📖 Did you catch the name of the book they tell you to find your final clue in?

📖 How can you shut the door to the fireplace?

📖 What happens when you enter the pattern from page **158** onto the door of the fireplace?

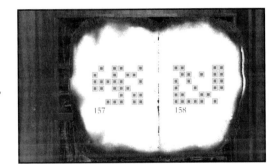

📖 After entering the correct pattern, is there anything else you must do to gain access to the secret chamber?

📖 What does the book do?

📖 Do you trust Sirrus, Achenar, or Atrus the most?

For the Solution to this mystery, turn to page **124**.

Finding the White Page

Atrus has requested a page for his book that will set him free from his prison.

📖 What did the two halves of the page, one half found in the Stoneship Age and the other in the Channelwood Age, say when placed together.

📖 Have you turned on all of the Marker Switches?

For the Solution to this mystery, turn to page **126**.

Entering D'ni

You now have the page that Atrus needs.

📖 How do you enter D'ni?

📖 What happens when you give Atrus the page he asks for?

For the Solution to this mystery, turn to page **127**.

Alternate Endings

If you don't want to give the page to Atrus, there are three alternate endings you may want to try.

What happens when you give one of the pages to the appropriate brother? Two of the alternate endings unfold if you give them their pages.

What happens when you visit Atrus without getting the White page for his book? This provides the third alternate ending.

For the Solution to this mystery, turn to page **129**.

The Solutions

After you have visited all of the Myst Ages, there is one last thing you must do. Each brother has asked you to retrieve a final page for his book, but without retrieving the other's page.

This is a good time to save your game, because there are two alternate endings that you may want to explore.

Entering the Fireplace

Both Achenar and Sirrus tell you to enter the fireplace and enter a specific pattern into the panel on the door.

📖 Go to the bookcase and pull the last book on the right from the middle shelf. Turn to page **158** and copy down the pattern you see there.

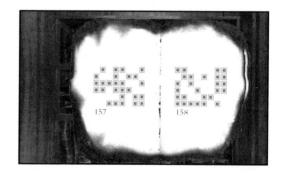

📖 Enter the fireplace, push the button on the left to shut the door, and enter the pattern onto the back of the door.

- 📖 Push the button again to turn the fireplace around and reveal a secret chamber with a Green book and Red and Blue pages.

- 📖 Don't take either page. Instead, pick up the Green book and open it. A new person is staring out at you from the pages of this book: it's Atrus, Sirrus and Achenar's father.

  Atrus wants you to place a page in a book that he has with him. You can assume that he doesn't mean the two pages below the book from which he is speaking.

- 📖 After Atrus has finished speaking, put down the book and return to the Library.

Finding the White Page

By this time you have scoured the entire island looking for clues to gain entry to the other Ages. There has been no page lying around for you to give to Atrus. The two halves of a sheet of paper—one found in the Stoneship Age, the other in Channelwood—provide the clue to the location of the final page.

📖 Make sure all of the Marker Switches on the island are turned on.

📖 Go to the Marker Switch on the dock and turn it off. A door opens in its base, revealing a White page.

Entering D'ni

You now have the page that Atrus spoke of. Returning it to him ends the game.

- 📖 Return to the fireplace. Shut the door, enter the pattern, and push the button to access the secret chamber.

- 📖 Pick up Atrus' book and touch his image. You are transported to the underground cavern of D'ni, Atrus' prison.

- 📖 Walk to him and when he asks, give him the White page.

Atrus leaves briefly to take care of his sons. When he returns, he says you are free to explore Myst Island and its various Ages at will, although he may need your help battling a greater foe than Achenar and Sirrus later on.

📖 Pick up the Myst book Atrus shows you and return to the Library. Both Achenar's and Sirrus' books have been destroyed.

You have completed the game and solved all of the Myst puzzles.

Alternate Endings

There are three alternate endings to the game that you may want to explore. Two are basically the same, differing only in which brother's page you replace.

Ending #1

- 📖 Restore the game you saved at the beginning of this chapter.

- 📖 Enter the fireplace and enter the pattern on the door.

- 📖 Pick up either the Red or Blue page.

- 📖 Return to the Library and put the page in the appropriate book.

  Doing so makes you switch places with either Achenar or Sirrus, and you become trapped while he is free to pillage all of the Myst Ages.

Ending #2

The third alternate ending occurs if you don't get the White page from the vault before visiting Atrus.

- Restore your saved game.

- Enter the fireplace and enter the pattern on the door.

- Pick up the Green book. Ignore Atrus' warning and touch his image to travel to D'ni.

- Atrus asks you for the page and, when he realizes that you don't have it, informs you that you and he are imprisoned there for eternity.

Appendix A

Troubleshooting

There's a four-page pamphlet included with each game that outlines a lot of the what-can-go-wrong-will-go-wrong situations in Myst. But who wants to wade through all that technical-ese? Here are the major problems the Broderbund technical support staff sees occurring to people playing this version of Myst.

Windows-Specific

☐ You should make sure you have updated your Myst program to version 1.01 (serial number #44962).

☐ Add or edit the "OPTIMIZE=" line in the video section of the QTW.INI file to "OPTIMIZE=BMP." This file is located in the Windows directory.

☐ Disable your "SMARTDRIVE" program in either your config.sys or autoexec.bat file by placing a "REM" or ";" command in front of the line and rebooting your system.

☐ Increase your Virtual Memory swap file to 10,000 and keep your Windows resources at 85 percent.

☐ Updating the device drivers for sound card, video card, and CD-ROM components resolves more than 90 percent of the problems people have with Myst. Hardware companies update these drivers at least every six months and usually much more frequently. You can get the drivers directly from the makers of your computer components.

Although there haven't been many problems reported while playing this version of the game, there are a few things you can do beforehand to avoid any potential problems. The following are the obstacles the technical support staff at Broderbund finds are most often encountered:

Macintosh-Specific

📖 Make sure you're using the 1.01 version of Myst (serial number #44602), and make sure you're using the Myst version of QuickTime (version 1.6.1 or greater) to run the program.

 If you're not, take the current version out of your extension folder, trash it, and then empty the trash. Reboot your Mac, and then put the Myst QuickTime into the folder. Also, make sure you take all the extensions out of your Extensions folder—with the exception of Sound Manager, your CD-ROM extension, and the Myst version of QuickTime—and place them into your Disabled Extensions folder. You must reboot your Mac for them to take effect.

📖 Make sure you don't have any control panels that might act as activated extensions, especially the Modern Memory Manager. Check which ones are active as extensions by looking in the task list of your Mac.

📖 Disable the Power Plug control panel when running Myst. (This doesn't apply to the Power Mac.)

📖 Change your preferred memory size to either 5,000 Kb or 6,000 Kb. You should also make sure your Disk Cache is set to 128 Kb.

📖 You should not be using any sort of auto-doubling or compression software with Myst.

Appendix B
Myst Online Resources

The World Wide Web is a great place to explore additional Myst mysteries. It's also an opportunity to catch up on gameplay information or get technical support. Some of the more helpful and popular online resources follow.

- **Cyan Home Page**

  http://www.cyan.com

- **Myst Walkthrough Plus**

  http://www.voicenet.com/~mmax/myst.html

- **Myst Hints and Tips**

  http://mindlink.net/peter_macdougall/myst.htm

- **Myst Technical Support**

  http://www.astro.washington.edu/ingram/myst/tech.html

- **Myst Island Help**

  http://www.astro.washington.edu/ingram/myst/myst.html

- **Technical Advisory**

  http://voicenet.com/~mmax/myst/techhelp.html

There are many other online resources available on Myst. Do not consider this a final list. If you have access to the Internet, take a couple of hours to find and explore other sites dedicated to Myst.

Usenet Groups

Usenet Newsgroups are good places to see what other Myst Players are doing and to ask specific questions about gameplay and any technical problems. What follows is an abbreviated list of some popular Usenet Newsgroups.

- comp.sys.mac.games

- bit.listserv.games-l

- comp.sys.ibm.pc.games.adventure

- comp.sys.ibm.pc.games.misc

- comp.sys.ibm.pc.soundcard.games

- comp.source.games

- comp.source.games.bugs

Also, you can explore forums on CompuServe, or check out the Game Information Exchange on America OnLine by searching for Myst or go to the Broderbund area by typing Keyword: Broderbund. And if that's not enough, try exploring the software libraries.

Other Strategy Guides Now Available from BradyGAMES
Order Toll Free
1-800-428-5331

Lands of Lore 2	1-56686-288-4	19.99
The Great Game	1-56686-425-9	19.99
Wing IV	1-56686-414-3	19.99
Beavis and Butthead Virtual Stupidity	1-56686-384-8	19.99
Cyber Chess	1-56686-386-4	19.99
Terra Nova	1-56686-349-X	19.99
Official Guide to Harvester	1-56686-290-6	19.99
Mechwarrior II	1-56686-191-8	19.99
Modem.Games	1-56686-298-1	19.99
Rec.Games	1-56686-311-2	19.99
On-Line Games	1-56686-275-2	19.99
Doom Super Book	1-56686-438-0	19.99
Terminal Velocity	1-56686-344-9	19.99
RPG Compendium	1-56686-340-6	19.99
Blaster Fun	1-56686-297-3	9.99
Totally Unauthorized Guide to 7th Guest/11th Hour	1-56686-192-6	19.99
Doom II	1-56686-228-0	19.99
Top Gun	1-56686-314-7	19.99
Myst Solutions	1-56686-313-9	7.99
X-Com 2: Terror From the Deep	1-56686-302-3	9.99
Origin Wing Commander 3	1-56686-287-6	19.99
Guide to Flight Simulator	1-56686-282-5	19.99
Solutions & Cheats to the Hottest PC Games	1-56686-277-9	19.99
Official Guide to Command and Conquer	1-56686-247-7	19.99
MUDs	1-56686-246-9	19.99
Doom	1-56686-187-X	9.95
Star Trek: A Final Unity	1-56686-207-8	19.99
Corridor 7	1-56686-219-1	19.99
Star Trek: Judgement Rites	1-56686-150-0	14.95
Return to Zork	1-56686-123-3	16.95
Sim City 2000	1-56686-205-1	19.99
The Lemmings Chronicles	1-56686-245-0	19.99
Tekken Pocket Guide	1-56686-441-0	7.99

Other Strategy Guides Now Available from BradyGAMES
Order Toll Free
1-800-428-5331

Secret of Evermore	1-56686-328-7	9.99
Doom Players Guide	1-56686-396-1	9.99
Killer Instinct SNES Pocket Guide	1-56686-419-4	7.99
The Toy Story Official Game Book	1-56686-447-X	9.99
Gargoyles Official Game Book	1-56686-442-4	9.99
Pocahontas Official Game Book	1-56686-390-2	9.99
Virtua Fighter Pocket Guide	1-56686-393-7	7.99
Judge Dredd Official Game Book	1-56686-370-8	9.99
Mortal Kombat 3 Pocket Codes	1-56686-381-3	7.99
Totally Unauthorized Guide to Primal Rage	1-56686-345-7	9.99
Sega Games Guide 2	1-56686-342-2	9.99
NBA Jam Tournament Edition Pocket Codes	1-56686-279-5	7.99
Fighting Games Secrets II	1-56686-317-1	9.99
Guide to Killer Instinct	1-56686-320-1	9.99
Mortal Kombat 3 Fighters Kompanion	1-56686-319-8	9.99
Donkey Kong Country 2 Secret Room Guide	1-56686-437-2	7.99
Donkey Kong Country 2	1-56686-318-X	9.99
Donkey Kong Country Secret Room Guide	1-56686-280-6	8.99
Killer Instinct Arcade Pocket Guide	1-56686-295-7	7.99
NBA Jam Tournament Edition Super Book	1-56686-293-0	19.99
Mortal Kombat 3 Arcade Secrets	1-56686-283-3	9.99
NBA Jam Tournament Edition Pocket Codes	1-56686-279-5	7.99

DESCEND INTO

///IBradyGAMES

BASEMENT

THESE AIN'T
NO REC ROOMS

PC GAME ROOM
- game shareware
- downloadable screen shots from the month's hottest games
- sample chapters of all the PC game guides
- game release lists updated weekly

VIDEO GAME ROOM
- downloadable screen shots from the month's hottest games
- sample chapters of popular video game strategy guides
- game release lists updated monthly
- new gaming tip featured daily, provided by Brady's gaming staff experts

JUNK TRUNK
- information on how to become a BradyGAMES author
- survey with chance to win strategy guides from BradyGAMES
- promotional updates
- ongoing contests

BRADY BUNCH ROOM
- meet the "cast" of BradyGAMES through pictures and profiles

SECRET ROOM
- get the most secret tips and exclusive news on gaming

http://www.mcp.com/brady